The Understor
52 sestudes on
by writers from

JENNI WALLACE | *Illustration*

I've always loved trees, but never thought about why. They are always there, part of our lives. In recent times, I've become more aware of my own ignorance, particularly as I was writing a novel, *The Good Messenger*, set in woods. The need to write about trees, and to be specific about them, grew a desire to find out more.

A meeting with the Woodland Trust was fortuitous. It opened up the opportunity to do something practical as I proposed a project '26 Trees' that would pair a writer from 26 with a species of tree. The Woodland Trust responded enthusiastically and here, almost magically less than a year later, is this book of poetic writing about trees.

26 is a membership collective of writers of many different kinds. They are mainly people who earn their living from writing in the business world. Projects such as this stretch them creatively and offer the opportunity to work in partnership with an organisation they admire and to engage with a subject that inspires.

And what an inspiration trees have been. We invited members to volunteer for the project and were overwhelmed by the response. As so many writers stepped forward, we decided to create two groups of 26 participants, making 52 writers in all.

Writers in the 'Core' group were each paired with a native UK tree, and the writers were chosen to reflect the national coverage of those trees. The 'Explore' group writers were free to choose trees outside that list. As writers in 'Explore' reflect 26's international membership, there are trees represented from different parts of the world.

The form each writer was asked to use is the sestude. This is '26 in reflection – 62 words exactly'. Within that tight word constraint you will see that there is potential for many different interpretations of form.

The writers' focus was trees, so they went into woods to embrace the principle of the Tree Charter: 'to celebrate the power of trees to inspire.' Through those visits, research, their own writing, they discovered more about trees – not least the need, in this climate emergency, to respect, conserve and plant trees for the sake of the world.

We all became aware that trees are now constantly in the news. While writing this foreword I read that the world loses an area of forest the size of the UK every year. This is a real emergency, particularly obvious in the Amazon but happening everywhere. We need to save trees and to plant trees.

Other news items interested me. I read that in Liverpool they've reopened Strawberry Field, with a new visitor centre for those who want to visit the inspiration for John Lennon's song. The article said that the trees Lennon climbed in his childhood are still there. Imagine. Trees outlive us, they remind us that we are just custodians for our short time on this earth. There's no need to imagine the real news from Denmark on the same day – through a telethon the Danish public has raised the funds to plant one million trees.

Every country needs to do the equivalent and trees might be the main means we have to combat climate change. Trees and people are allies. Perhaps the main feeling experienced by all the writers involved was a sense of connection – with their tree, with other individuals, with the planet, with their own identity.

Perhaps this is what the poet Lemn Sissay meant when he wrote in his recent autobiography about writing his first poem: "In writing about the tree, I wrote about myself."

I commend this book to you. And I thank all the writers who contributed to it and our partners at the Woodland Trust who made it happen.

JOHN SIMMONS | Co-Founder of 26

Most of our lives unfold close to trees. Our journeys to work and the shops, our weekend walks, teenage romances and texted exchanges all take place under the watchful gaze of trees.

It's easy to take trees for granted, but they are a living link with our past, as special in their way as the artworks in our galleries or books in our libraries.

Thousands of years ago, glaciers covered Britain during the Ice Age. As they melted and retreated, trees colonised the empty landscape that was left behind. Fast forward ten thousand years, and the trees that line our streets and grow in our gardens, parks and woods are their direct descendants. The birches and oaks that once watched over animals like wolves and bears are here with us now, generations on – bearing witness to our lives. Part of our family tree.

Trees are our past – and they are our future, too. A new mass effort to plant trees and let them grow in unprecedented numbers across our landscapes will be one of our best lines of defence for saving humanity in a rapidly warming world. As they grow, trees store carbon in their leaves, branches, trunks and roots. Every tree counts and every tree makes a difference.

The challenge for those of us who care about trees is how to help everyone else notice them, reflect on what they do for us. And to encourage people to do what they can to protect them, or plant more.

This is the challenge that the writers in this book have taken on.

One group of 26 writers has focused on a species of tree native to Britain – hornbeam, birch, oak, ash and many others. They have lived with that tree, tried to understand it and unpick its essence, so that it can be shared and understood by others. Then, another group of 26 has explored trees not necessarily native to Britain, because we recognise that this is an issue that is both local and global.

This project was inspired by the Tree Charter – a modern-day version of the 800-year old Charter of the Forest. The Charter was first created in 1217 to protect people's right to access forests for timber and food. In 2017, the Woodland Trust led a partnership project to create a new Charter for Trees, Woods and Peoples to reflect the relationship we have now with trees. We were once dependent on trees for almost everything in our lives – food, shelter, building materials. And now, in an age of climate crisis, a new dependency exists.

We are immensely grateful to the 26 writers' group for choosing to write about trees. I hope you enjoy the results.

ADAM CORMACK | Head of Campaigning | the Woodland Trust

COMMON DOES YOU NO JUSTICE ALDER

Well,
at least maddened Sweeney
had a good word to say for you:
'Delightful is thy hue'.

Tell that to the spirits
of dead warriors; their heads,
stained yellow by catkins,
adorning your branches.

Cut your flesh
and white
turns red.

Anti-Christ
to the Tree of Life,
listen to what men say.
Watch them
turn in fear
to find another way home.

TOM COLLINS | *Alder* | Stirling, Scotland

YNYS ENLLI APPLE TREE

Flat to the salt hewn brick,
The Mother tree calls
Into the lighthouse's foghorn yawn,
Past the watercolour sea.

She's older than the last islander
And the lobsters on the wall.
Fat with bonemeal of bards,
Who fled in boats to pray and die.

Now. City kids splashed with muck,
Kick up shingle,
And spit the pips
Of your small, rare fruit.

KATIE ALCOCK | *Apple* | north Wales

ASH

They say the sky-god bleeds
and ashes fall
in a rain of keys

They say this one's old
or ugly or dead
or unsightly

They say there's no reason why
she stands upright
when you can climb inside
to where time carved out her heart

She says nothing

heartlessly alive

300 summers high

reaching every brand new leaf
back beyond the sky

JULIA FOX | *Ash* | Northants

ASPEN

you tremble as if on the brink of
                                        something
my father would love your smooth bark
white as bone
would run his maker's fingers
over its braille
imagining   oar   shield   box

aspen
    your saffron leaves quake
    each shimmer a tiny semaphore

    I will sew a wild and leafy crown
    dive into your rootworld's dark fusion
    rise with unshed secrets on my tongue

SUE BURGE | *Aspen* | Norfolk

BEECH (FAGUS SYLVATICA)

I can't creep up on you Beech Tree,
You hear me scrunch through decades of
    disintegrated nuts and mast.
Were I limber I would clamber to the crook of
    your elephant skinned arm.
Rather, looking skyward through
    fractyl shimmer green, my fingers
    making wishes in the tracery of bark
I listen;
A breath of wind,
And I hear tree instead of me.

JEANNIE MACLEAN | *Beech* | Angus, Scotland

BLACKTHORN WINTER

I am no sunlit briar: my thorns
are long and septic-sharp.
I hold out bare arms –
their black wounds visible –
I am an expert at self-harm.

I can endure a thousand winters
till I thaw – in my belly
stones from my blue sloes
I dried to cure my ailments
and bring me over the mountain.
I carry my own healing.

JUSTINA HART | *Blackthorn* | Staffordshire

RHAMNUS CATHARTICA

Ingleton, Delamere
Hay, Dean
Road trips
Boat trips
Hikes

Broken but looking up
Scarce and still unseen.

Here's our time
to explore

Memories of scuffed knees
and swinging from trees.

Heady days
Hearty grub

These days are theirs
I lead by example

unleashed
Through the undergrowth and scrub.

Yomping. Stomping.
Crashing. Splashing.
Releasing my inner child.

Still looking.
Until then, reconnected.
Wild.

CLARE JENNINGS | *Buckthorn* | Cheshire

DOGWOOD

Don't define me, as you try and control
and restrict me. I will not be ignored. I will
not go unnoticed. Lost in the green of my
companions? Wait until winter, when I will
display my crimson rage. You see me now? I
am different. I can stand alone. Independent.
Male? Female? I am neither, yet I am both.
Don't define me.

ERICA REID | *Dogwood* | Galashiels, Scotland

DRIFT, WOOD

Hiding in plain sight, nettle-bound at a
  crossroads
Some flowers remain, drifting like smoke on
  dead fire
Brash berry buds hang from fragile fingers
Elder Mother is resting, waiting
As frothy frills float gently past

To revel in love's joyful, bright flame
All that remains are heaped beach cinders and
Discarded memories of the night before
Stirred up by the salty breeze

LAURA CLAY | *Elder* | central Scotland

SEVEN SISTERS

Taiko drums warble
And babble
As the forest nymphs
Cavalcade down the mountain
To take their place around
Old mighty always.
'Perennial seven. Forgotten, twisted sisters.
Form the arboreal belt for
The belly of the heavens'.

Our dead king spinning a knife
In his fingers steps inside.
He cuts the surface
And places a walnut
In the scarred earth
Before they sing.

JAMIE DELVES | *Elm* | Seven Sisters, London

IN RICHMOND PARK
A HAZEL 'TREE'

Interloper
Shrub
Bush
Overgrown weed

They might be right
The oaks you see

I'm short
Slim limbed
But twice as smart
As our national tree

People here
Take snaps of the deer
But Hermes the Messenger
Focused on me

So can you blame me
For being angry
When the ancients worshipped me?

Hazel
They cried
The gods surely bless
The Knowledge Tree

ANDY HAYES | *Hazel* | southwest London

LADY-IN-WAITING

Overshadowed by gossiping poplars,
crowded by muttering oaks,
in Lagan Meadows
I almost disregard you.

Your jagged skirt keeps me at boughs' length –
any closer and you will scratch.
I kneel at your hem,
note supple, green arms,
the scoop and point of leaf edges,
clusters of green berries
embroidered like seed pearls
across satin.

Deep within I sense a kingdom ripening.

LUCY BEEVOR | *Holly* | Northern Ireland

A FOOT STEPS FROM THE ORIENTAL HORNBEAM

In a Belfast park,
bug bitten beneath your sprawl
I crawl inside you

guessing the twist grew
from root to shoot to sapling,
looped up, out, sprouting

double edged sharp tongues,
trails of soft green tresses flung,
hiding pock-marked skin,

my cracked fissures yours,
your gobbled body parts mine,
all stretched, split, lived, lined,

contortionist's limbs
thrown akimbo must reveal
a hidden wishbone.

THERESE KIERAN | *Hornbeam* | Belfast

JUNIPER SKY ROCKET

A queen and her baby
joey in pouch

Afraid
alone in motherhood

Persevering assailant sky, taller now,
forced up too young

At night the moon sings
to your subtle hum, your baby crying

Hushed lullaby 'til the stars burn out
and the horizon fast knows dawn

New direction? Paris?
I'm not sure Juniper.

I'll keep you company,
yes. Thank you for asking.

ALEX MAWSON-HARRIS | *Juniper* | Cornwall

COMMON/PRIVATE

Paired, my trees mark gates of the old workhouse
(now private residential streets, like many)
surround themselves with (I've just learned this word)
suckers – new growth that gardeners control.
Their bark is grey. Not photo grey but live,
gnarled and with recent branches offering
leaves greenfly have holed. The trees stand tall,
one bent. The tree book keeps them with X rating.

AIDAN BAKER | *Lime* | Cambridgeshire

THE MAJOR

You,
in a forest of oaks
are the Major Oak,
myth heavy,
fat with tales,
trunk pitted
boughs bowed,
strutted,
but not strutting.

We,
come,
park,
look,
walk about,
picnic,
take a pic,
leave.

You,
have rooted,
harboured jackdaws
and outlaws

befriended robins,
and Robin Hoods,
nurtured starlings
and stories,
become a legend,
yourself,
grown leaves,
shed leaves,
for
eleven
hundred
years.

MARTIN LEE | *Oak* | Nottinghamshire

PEAR

Dedicated to goddesses, a tree of life, I bring fecundity, fertility, fidelity when planted.

Symbol of immortality and togetherness for Ancient Chinese, my sweet flesh never divided to avoid separations.

'A gift from the gods'*, my heavy fruits promise newborns' safe birth, growth, longevity.

My female cults as rare as my wild genus, cultivars carried by corsairs and missionaries propagate the world.

* Homer

IRENE LOFTHOUSE | *Pear* | Yorkshire

PLANE TALE FROM THE CITY

Once
you came on a
flying visit
borne on a high wind
from Spain
a secret agent
a migrant.
You stayed. You became
more London than Londoners
losing your accent
adopting a cockney swagger
hiding in plain sight
a model native.
Your otherness unnoticed now
your bark camouflaged in khaki.
You fit in
cityslicker.

This tree
always will be
you and me.

JOHN SIMMONS | *Plane* | north London

TO KNOW

What is a tree?
A tree, my love
Makes wind true
Hands peace a voice
Reveals the day
Through half-light
Kind fracture
Of dappled leaves
And a sort-of-quiet
In your roaring soul.
Here where light
Drenches green.
The heavy moon
Drips through
Tangled branches
Like blackened snow.
What is a tree?
It is time, my love
Skittish, scattered
Stippled time.
Hold still.

ELEN LEWIS | *Poplar* | Dorset

THE RED THREAD

"I've been waiting for you"
says young Rowan,
"the calendar winds said you would come,
salt air spoke your voice".

Red, the essence of berries
and Beltane Fire.[1]

Protection.

Rowan, devoured by the Tuatha dé Danann.[2]
Keeping cattle safe, the core of watermill pins
and red-tied twigs.

Your glow bathes me with
red-green, light and fruitfulness.

"together we stand rosy with love".

1 J.G. Frazer (1922), the Golden Bough, MacMillan & Co, London.
2 F. M. McNeill (1956), The Silver Bough, MacLellan, Edinburgh

SANDY WILKIE | *Rowan* | Argyll, Scotland

"WE HAVE NOT JUST PLANTED A WOODLAND, WE ARE WATCHING AN IDEA GROW."

From relict Caledonian forest:
The seed of an idea
The pride of a community.

Rising from the ashes:
A humble lichen-clad survivor
A steadfast watchman of the Way
A child of the millennium.

Rooted in a landscape shaped by glaciers
    and memories
Just a cone's throw away
From the scars of lead
From battles and clearances
A new story is growing.

SOPHIE GORDON | *Scots Pine* | Scotland

THE SILVER BIRCH

Higher!

I push because I'm littler,
And she told me to.

I toil in the shade,
Her toes reach the sun.

A silver effort,
She's the golden one.

Two buds, same branch,
Knots of upwards adoration.

But today she's mean.
I'm gnarled.
I forget to look up to her.
Everything twists, she falls.
Breaks.
Dad roars.

I pray our roots are strong.

JESSICA SWALES | *Silver Birch* | Somerset

SPINDLE

Whorl, drop, draw.
Fingers tease,
Lips release,
Gravity's pull transforms soft chaos.

A scrubby shrub.
The purge and goad of beasts
But I keep winter robins fed.

Prickwood draws blood,
Spell cast,
The world turns.

From swaddle to shroud,
On the niddy-noddy of fortune,
I sketch your fate.
The heart wood of your fibre,
I've spun you every yarn.
Whorl, drop, draw.

Glossary

whorl – a spiral or circular pattern, also the weighted part of a drop spindle.

prickwood – another common name for the spindle tree.

niddy-noddy – a tool used to make skeins from yarn.

MICHELLE NICOL | *Spindle* | Northumberland

WHITEBEAM

A boy walked in the woods after dark. He was
scared. Even more so when he saw a dark
shape. Just as he turned to run, the shape
lit a torch and the torch lit the leaves of the
Whitebeam tree. And in the beautiful canopy
of light he saw his father standing there. And
forevermore the tree was his secret comfort.

STEVE BOYLE | *Whitebeam* | Liverpool

PATRIARCH

A bald crown, sideways stoop, shattered limbs:
This old boy could go at any time,
Collapsing into his twin's outstretched arms as
    his gnarled heart cracks.

But until the fall he'll give life.
Ducks nest in his hollows, bees mine his
    catkins, ferns sprout green in every furrow,
And each spring his seed drifts across the
    wetland acres, growing the family tree.

REBECCA DOWMAN | *Willow* | Sussex

HOLLOWING

In this tree I first forgot you
For a fair-haired child
Who climbed before me.

He held a secret to be hidden
In the looming
Hollow yew.

Soon he left the churchyard, glowing
Blessed lifelong
By the golden bloom.

That's when I stole from him this sorrow
And heavy hearted
Hid it higher, out of reach,
To spare him from tomorrow's gloom.

SAMUEL MOSELEY WEBB | *Yew* | south Wales

OLD APPLE

For eighty years it stood
Weathered, withered
At the far end of our garden,
Keeping watch.

Three dead arms and one good one
Reaching out:
Knuckles thick and joints gnarled,
Bark-hard touch like working palms.

Doing what it did
With all it had:
One branch of blossom,
One string of buds.

And the little apples
When we bit.
How fresh,
How sweet.

DAVID MANDERSON | *Apple* | Giffnock, Glasgow

THE GRAVEYARD ASH

I'm watching you.
Meeting. Singing. Canoodling. Arguing.
You're small, but infinitely beautiful.

I yearn to run. To hold hands. To leap.

Tree of life, they once called me. But my
  roots are firmly fixed in the earth; where
  they tangle through skulls and twist
  twixt bones.

Dust to dust.

Three forgotten boys rot beneath me. And
  I will embrace them for eternity.

SUZIE INMAN | *Ash* | Helston, Cornwall

DAY'S END AND THE BANANA TREE, JAKARTA (AKHIR HARI DAN POHON PISANG, JAKARTA)

Wearied light pushes the thick air
past competing calls to prayer
and motorway roar

while stub-tailed cats stalk the pseudo-stems,
velcro-pawed geckos sprint up spines
of new growth, lemon-green,

and older wind-frayed fronds droop
as heat grinds breath between its hands.

Dusk's handover overhead
of swifts to bats' neat flip and swerve,
to sudden black,
stars haze-hidden.

Headlights strobe
the upheld pennons.

JOAN LENNON | *Banana* | Jakarta

THE TWT* BEECH

I have watched the see-saw of lives
  across time.

First, the dare-you children scaling
  my steely stem
To swing,
Carefree,
Carelessly,

In my limbs.

Later, one another's loves:
Careful seeding,
Nourished, flourishing
Dashed.

Sawn: I am down, but not gone.
I have been so much, to so many.

In all these lives, I live on
And on
And on.

*Welsh: small, colloq.

JO AARON LILFORD | *Beech* | Cowbridge, Wales

HIGHER CONSCIOUSNESS

It amused my daughters that a town in distant south-east England shared the name we gave their favourite tree.

We never went there, which is probably just as well.

I don't mean that cruelly: but with its startling protuberance, blending nature's wonderful perversity with the feel of low-budget sci-fi dystopia, no town could ever hope to capture the essence of . . .

The Braintree.

STEPHEN BARNABY | *Braintree* |
Lewisvale Park, Musselburgh

THE STRONG AND SENSITIVE TYPE

I made my mark on them.
Impressed by centuries, catkins and burs,
The Borough of Stockport named a street
   for me,
And declared they would
Preserve my wood
From deliberate harm.

They made their mark on me.
Two lovers scratched each other
Into my smooth, steel-grey bark;
My gargantuan stature scarred
By their passion.
I wear their hearts on my silvery sleeve.

ROWENA ROBERTS | *Common Beech* |
Stockport, Lancashire

FAMILY TREE

Three children, from days gone
mouths stretched wide in glee
Scattered, posing for the camera
    on the ancient cypress
Rugged and old, a bold and brave being
Solid and strong in form
Gnarled trunk stands tall
Branches stretched out in disarray
A canopy of thirsty leaves in the basking sun
A photo of a memory
A tree where family happiness is found

FRANCESCA BAKER | *Cypress* | Malta

DAKPLATAAN,
NORTH HOLLAND

Back in April   you seemed almost dead:
smooth   skeleton starfish balancing
              on a
              single foot

Stretching four
                    perpendicular arms
towards the horizon,
                    cropped
fingers straining
to
touch
the
sky

June draws out your digits. A roof appears
for cats to lounge
under.
You finger the glowing hem of the night.
How tense are your arms with the green
wind
in
your
sails
?

SABINE HARNAU | *Dakplataan* | Netherlands

THE LAST OLD ELM

You stand

Raking skywards

As generations
To and fro
To and fro
Absorbed in daily busyness

You feel
The gentle tamping of feet
Asphalt vibrations

You see all
Mostly unnoticed
Watching over life at the Dials

You stood tall
When threatened with council axe
People scaled your branches
Wreathed you in words

Save our tree.

Until, finally, a reprieve.

Still
You stand.

HEATHER ATCHISON | *Elm* | Seven Dials, Brighton

GULMOHAR

Summer's fierce height and
the streets are empty at noon.
The air here is warmer than blood
when you bloom, peacock tree.
Chilli bright blossoms on ashen bark,
crimson flowers fall stark upon
tired earth to bless the dead who call
from their tombs. Seeds split in forest
fires, life bursts from embers. You rise
again a flaming bird, red as myth.

GITA RALLEIGH | *Gulmohar* | Delhi, India

THE CREATION

In a hollow, heeled to the wind
bowling in from the Atlantic,
a stout tree crouches
as if cast adrift.

Bent backed,
its gnarled knotty spine exposed.
A tangle of thorny branches shore up
the sharp green canopy,
sprawling in endless bad hair days.

Wind tossed tendrils
curve
towards another:

tufty
small
upright.

In the lee of its spread
their fingertips
touch.

JULIA WEBB-HARVEY | *Hawthorn* |
Penhale Sands, north Cornwall

PILGRIMS

The original pilgrim
stalks the retreating ice,
trailed by a carpet of crack-nuts,
a treasure map
to the threshold between worlds

as long-dead Saxon drovers
march to the beat of the hammer pond,
with wind-tumbled pollen at their backs
and wisdom wedged in the coppice stools.

Weary, the tooth-leaved traveller dozes
long enough for a hazel
dormouse to call a hollow home.

LISA ANDREWS | *Hazel* | High Weald, Kent

LORD OF THE FOREST'S LAMENT

The sky is my Father.
My mother, earth.
I grew up to let light between forest
   and cloud.
My brother made the ocean his home.
But we share the same scaled skin.
You took to my family with blade and
   fire and steel.
Dragged them to your houses and ships.
The tide is turning.
Wring your hands
while our wounds weep ambergris.

JANE BERNEY | *Kauri* | New Zealand

AT THE MARGINS

Along the valley, glacier
receding beyond, icefall crack
cuts the wind whispering
the past that trodden
underbrush gives up

Larch bursts spring leaves
a spritz in the margins,
and quivers towards summer.

Autumn glow will give no winter
canopy but cones firm to the branch,
promised up for the years

And all around, your futures: cradling
windfall, or ghosted
in weathered buildings

DAVID BATY | *Larch* | Haute-Savoie, France

TREE OF LIFE

A muster of fowl on every branch
A Babel of tongues whistle and clatter
Around my destroyer of sorrow

One foot rooted in the underworld
hands thrown high – to the edge of heaven
Its sacred canopy my cathedral

Triple roots entwine my heart
And calm my mind
Balm to my sleepless soul

Axis mundi:
the still point around which
my world turns

ED PRICHARD | *Of Life* | The Garden of Eden

THE GOLDEN AGE OF THE FICUS MACROPHYLLA*

Through pale-moon filtered
branches drifts a chorus of golden fluid
    syllables: the Guadalquivir
streaming into Atlantic mist.
Arboreal sail-shrouds lie furled,
mainmast weeps no more,
coagulation cascading over time, sealing in
    the lucrative serum latex.
A shady past, first kiss, last sob.

Yeasty briny spores seeping from under the
    veil of Flor,
nut-dryness dripping onto chlorophyl-green
    leaf, dropping like stone onto ochre-red
    ground.

*Known locally as the giant rubber trees of Cadiz

PAUL MURPHY | *Moreton Bay Fig* | Andalucia

WITHIN

Fern's filigree, looping lianes,
wintry light through waving leaves.
Dappled, wild-beaten, generous bark,
tīekes' flutter-dance around.

Giant roots in earthbound fuse,
thick-skinned, craggy, centuries' crease.
Sunlit sway far above,
distant rustle, distant blue.

Plunder, clearance, roar and scream,
thunderous crash, gnawing teeth,
eyes-shut sigh as millennia fall,
ghosts in the hollow of your slow embrace.

Rātānui.

Here.

Still.

JAYNE WORKMAN | *Northern Rata* | New Zealand

THE INSIDER

We were loyal fans: us ancient oaks.
We loved watching them play.
But one day a sorry defender crossed
    the pitch,
And climbed into our eldest's arms to say:

"They're coming for you."

Her whispered words stirred the bats,
startled the butterflies,
set the birds gossiping anew.

We looped roots and swayed together,
just like forever.
But oh, how we trembled, too.

ROSE RADTKE | *Oak* |
Upper Dicker, Low Weald, East Sussex

THE AIR WE BREATHE

Wanting a view, we uprooted you
Found you a corner, then heard your bark
   whisper:
"As I fight for the light that my absence
   lets through
And the heat's bittersweet on the land
   where I grew
Do you ever wonder what you couldn't see
Something that's bigger than one olive tree?
Careless selfish foolish reckless
Let me die I'll leave you breathless."

SOPHIE OLSZOWSKI | *Olive* | Lyme Regis

CRACKED FOUNDATIONS

White man proclaimed the state by the
Old Gum Tree, though the Kaurna were
there long before. He spread out along
the mighty Murray, using redgum to build
houses, farms, communities.

Now the redgums are stressed, branches
falling; the river, dying. Gumnut babies
for generations past; grey-green leaves in
ceramic form only.

Things change – they must. But not like
this.

LAUREN McMENEMY | *River Redgum* | South Australia

BROUGHT TO EARTH

They've cut down our protector
We didn't mean they should –
But broken on the lawn they piled
Cross-cuts of rowan wood.

A flying rowan this one,
Its double dose of charm
Defended us from evils past:
What form the future harm?

We planted there another.
To renew the ancient spell -
But every fall I ask if
Yellow berries work as well.

STEPHEN POTTS | *Rowan* | Lauder, Berwickshire

I COULD HAVE BEEN
A CONTENDER ...

I might have been a cathedral beam,
the keel and prow of a plunging galleon,
a sturdy crooked house frame.
I might have been so useful
but for growing on this little hill,
unnoticed by builders and makers.

So since the world shunned me
I grew into my own world,
a habitat for plants and creatures,
I am their source of life.

VIVIEN JONES | *Sessile Oak* | Scotland

A SYCAMORE IN
THE ASYLUM PARK

It was meant to be a humane place.
They even planted trees.
One looks like the spirit of the madhouse
   has entered it,
As it twists away from the light.
Did it comfort the lunatics
To see their agonies reflected in its
   thrashing limbs?
And now, does it comfort the new residents
   of the old asylum,
The one-hit-wonders and oligarchs'
   abandoned mistresses?

ROGER MORRIS | *Sycamore* | Colney Hatch, London

IN TARZAN TREE

beyond Goosegog Bush,
we crunch cola cubes
and dangle like catkins
in sharp-toothed leaves.
Lighter than cuckoo spit
and woozy on crew cut lawn,
we pinwheel through wicker
until our socks scuff sage
or we hear your Dinner! rap on glass.

In the twist of our willow

~ in the moss and the muck ~
we wonder:
are you watching now?

GEMMA CANTELO | *Willow* | Kiamarie, Elstree

WITCH'S BROOM

Lost lovers once etched a heart around
their initials. Your reply: to graft.

To annul, unhurriedly. And breathe.

And to weave.

The villagers named you, perceiving a skull
sculpted from your lattice of vines and
gyrating branches.

We always impress our fleeting identities
onto you. You pay no notice. Our
generations become your breaths, each
moulding air into tangled arbour and
heartwood.

PHILIP PARKER | *Witch's Broom* |
Abinger Hammer, Surrey

THE OLD MAN
OF THE WOODS

Some call it the Old Man of the Woods.
For others, it's the Magic Tree –
a thousand-year-old guardian
with the power to grant your heart's desire.

Many seek it, fewer find it.
The forest shifts,
paths disappear.
Even those who know leaf, bark and berry
become lost.

Should you discover it,
step close, palm to gnarled trunk.
What would you wish for?

FIONA EGGLESTONE | *Yew* | Beaulieu, New Forest

First published in 2019
by 26 Characters Ltd
5 Cromwell Place
London SW7 2JE

ISBN 978-1-9162665-0-6

British Library Cataloguing in Publication Data.
A catalogue record for this book is available from
the British Library.

Designed by David Carroll & Co
Edited by Lisa Andrews
Typeface *Charter* by Matthew Carter
Illustration by Jenni Wallace